# YO-YO MA

### By Susan Ashley

WORLD ALMANAC® LIBRARY

**Please visit our web site at: www.worldalmanaclibrary.com**
**For a free color catalog describing World Almanac® Library's list**
**of high-quality books and multimedia programs, call 1-800-848-2928 (USA)**
**or 1-800-387-3178 (Canada). World Almanac® Library's fax: (414) 332-3567.**

Library of Congress Cataloging-in-Publication Data

Ashley, Susan.
    Yo-Yo Ma / by Susan Ashley.
        p. cm. — (Trailblazers of the modern world)
    Includes bibliographical references and index.
    ISBN 0-8368-5497-7 (lib. bdg.)
    ISBN 0-8368-5266-4 (softcover)
    1. Ma, Yo-Yo, 1955—Juvenile literature.  2.  Violoncellists—Biography—Juvenile
literature.  I. Title.  II. Series.
ML3930.M11A85   2004
787.4'092—dc22
[B]                                                    2004041294

First published in 2005 by
**World Almanac® Library**
330 West Olive Street, Suite 100
Milwaukee, WI 53212 USA

Copyright © 2005 by World Almanac® Library.

Project manager: Jonny Brown
Editor: Jim Mezzanotte
Design and page production: Scott M. Krall
Photo research: Diane Laska-Swanke
Indexer: Walter Kronenberg

Photo credits: © Evan Agostini/Getty Images: 5; © Carlo Allegri/Getty Images: 24 top; © AP/Wide World Photos: cover, 4, 6, 29, 36, 38, 40, 41, 43; © Fitzroy Barrett/Globe Photos: 7; © Bettmann/CORBIS: 14, 15, 17, 24 bottom; © Jerry Cooke/Time Life Pictures/Getty Images: 18; © William Coupon/CORBIS: 25; © Nigel J. Dennis; Gallo Images/CORBIS: 26; © Bill Eppridge/Time Life Pictures/Getty Images: 16; © Nathan Farb/Time Life Pictures/Getty Images: 19; © Robert Holmes/CORBIS: 20; © Hulton Archive/Getty Images: 10, 11; © Cynthia Johnson/Time Life Pictures/Getty Images: 27; Scott M. Krall/© World Almanac Library, 2005: 33; © Bob Krist/CORBIS: 13; © David Lees/CORBIS: 8; © Philippa Lewis; Edifice/CORBIS: 22; © Darren McCollester/Getty Images: 21; © Wally McNamee/CORBIS: 30; © Richard Melloul/CORBIS SYGMA: 31 top; © Viviane Moos/CORBIS: 37; © Javier Pierini/CORBIS: 31 bottom; © Patrick Robert/CORBIS SYGMA: 34; © Milan Ryba/Globe Photos: 39; © Moshe Shai/CORBIS: 32; © Joseph Sohm; ChromoSohm Inc./CORBIS: 12

Printed in the United States of America

1 2 3 4 5 6 7 8 9 08 07 06 05 04

# TABLE of CONTENTS

Words that appear in the glossary are printed in **boldface**
type the first time they occur in the text.

# CHAPTER 1

# CELEBRITY CELLIST

When Yo-Yo Ma performs, he wants his listeners to be excited by the music they hear.

In a darkened concert hall, ten musicians sit at the front of the stage. They begin playing, and the hall is filled with haunting melodies. The high notes of a flute, the shimmer of a cymbal, and the lush sounds of a cello all paint an exotic landscape. The music was written by Dmitri Yanov-Yanovsky, a modern-day composer from the Central Asian country of Uzbekistan. Although the concert hall is in the United States, cellist Yo-Yo Ma and his fellow musicians transport the audience to the faraway plains of the composer's home country.

When Yo-Yo Ma performs, he leads his audience on a journey— a journey of the imagination. Whether interpreting the music of Beethoven or a young composer from Uzbekistan, Ma wants his listeners to be moved by what they hear. He is not interested in simply playing the notes as they appear on paper. Those notes represent the experiences and emotions of the composer, which Ma wants to communicate to his audience.

Ma communicates using his whole body. He doesn't just play the cello—he embraces it. When there is speed or tension in the music, Ma leans forward, his brow furrowed in deep concentration. When the music relaxes, he leans back, eyes closed, all tension gone. You can almost hear the music just by watching his facial expressions. Ma does not look at his cello when he plays. He watches the conductor or his fellow musicians, urging them on with a quick nod or a smile. Ma smiles often when he performs. Audiences have the impression that he is enjoying the music as much as they are—and he is!

## Ignoring Gravity

When Yo-Yo Ma performs, his concentration is intense. Once, while playing in Philadelphia, his chair tipped over. As Ma fell backward, the audience gasped. A musician behind Ma caught him just in time. Amazingly, Ma kept playing through all of it and sat back down without missing a beat.

## A HUMBLE STAR

Yo-Yo Ma is the most famous cellist in the world. His celebrity status is on the same level as that of a rock star or a famous athlete. Thanks to his appearances on children's television programs, he is as popular with children as he is with adults. Ma has won sixteen Grammy Awards and recorded over fifty albums. He has appeared as a soloist with most of the major symphony orchestras in the world. He is a true superstar, but one would never know it upon meeting him. Ma is soft-spoken and humble.

Yo-Yo Ma has won sixteen Grammy Awards. His awards reflect the range of musical styles he has explored, from traditional classical music to tango, Appalachian, and Brazilian music.

Yo-Yo Ma's popularity won him a star on the Tower Records walk of fame in Boston, Massachusetts.

He says of himself, "I'm just a performing musician." When people come to his concerts, Ma hopes it is the music that draws them and not his fame. As he once told an interviewer, "The concept of superstardom can, in fact, lessen the experience for the listener. If someone goes to a concert only for the name of the performer, he may be less aware of the music itself, and not trust himself to open up to the real musical experience, on whatever level it may be."

## At Home on Stage

Many musicians get nervous playing before an audience. Yo-Yo Ma is completely relaxed. Ma has always felt comfortable on stage, even as a child. He once said, "When I perform, I have this image of people who have been invited into my living room and we're sharing something." Ma is famous for his informality—even in a tuxedo, he appears casual and easygoing—as well as for his impulse to share. Ma wants to bring music to the world. Even when he is onstage, he sees no barrier between himself and the audience. When it comes to music, everyone is participating.

Many people are unfamiliar with classical music. It is not as popular as other kinds of music, such as rock and pop. But with his informal stage manner, his frequent concert appearances, and his numerous recordings — including soundtracks to a number of popular movies — Yo-Yo Ma has brought classical music to a much wider audience.

It is rare for a cellist — even a **virtuoso** like Yo-Yo Ma — to become a household name. Part of the reason is the cello's **repertoire**. In classical music, the cello's repertoire is much smaller than that of other instruments, such as the piano or the violin. Ma has worked to change that. He has **commissioned** many new pieces for the cello, particularly from American composers. He has also broadened people's knowledge of the

Ma pushed musical boundaries in 2003 when he recorded an album of Brazilian music. Pictured here are pianist Kathryn Stott (center) and singer and guitarist Rosa Passos (right), who joined Ma for the recording session and a series of concert tours.

# The Soulful Cello

The cello is a very expressive instrument. It produces a deep, rich, and soothing sound. Some people have compared the **range** of the cello to that of the human voice. The cello is a string instrument. Like the violin, it has four strings that produce sound when they are plucked or when a bow is drawn across them. The cello is much larger than the violin, however, and its range extends to a much lower **pitch**. To play the cello, a cellist sits and holds the instrument upright. The bottom of the cello rests on a metal spike and the top leans against the cellist's shoulder.

Some of the finest cellos ever made were handcrafted in Italy during the eighteenth century. Today, they are worth millions of dollars. Yo-Yo Ma plays two Italian cellos—a Davidoff Stradivarius made in 1712 and a Montagnana made in Venice in 1733. Once, in 1999, Ma accidentally left the Montagnana cello in the trunk of a New York City taxi cab! The cello was valued at $2.5 million. Fortunately, Ma had kept his taxi receipt. He was able to track the car down to a garage in the city and recover the cello.

In addition to his two older, Italian cellos, Ma plays modern cellos, including a radical new instrument called a hypercello. The hypercello uses technology to enhance the sound and performance of a traditional cello. It is connected to a computer, and sensors on the instrument allow the computer to measure and quickly respond to every move the cellist makes.

Students learn to make classical instruments at a school in Cremona, Italy. Cremona has been a center of fine instrument-making since the sixteenth century. The city was home to Antonio Stradivari, whose violins and cellos are among the most prized in the world.

existing repertoire by playing lesser-known classical pieces from the twentieth century.

But Yo-Yo Ma's accomplishments extend far beyond the world of classical music. Ma has used the cello to popularize many other musical styles as well. Playing everything from Appalachian folk music to South American tangos, he has reinvented the way people think of the cello. It is no longer an instrument reserved for the symphony orchestra; it is at home in a variety of musical settings.

Ma's musical adventures have gained him fans all over the world — and all over the musical spectrum. People who once may have listened only to classical music may now be listening to Brazilian music, thanks to Yo-Yo Ma. Likewise, people who never listened to classical music are more likely to go to a classical concert if they know Ma is performing. It is not just Ma's fame that draws them, nor his extraordinary talent as a musician. Ma's warmth and enthusiasm have much to do with his popularity. As a reporter once wrote, "This youthful Chinese-American galloped on stage with a smile that could have melted icebergs. Before he played a note, he had his audience captivated."

Yo-Yo Ma's fame, talent, and reputation as a performer have both increased the popularity of classical music and exposed his audiences to new musical worlds. Ma has taken the cello, and his fans, from Bach to **bossa nova** — and beyond.

## The World of Classical Music

What is classical music? Strictly speaking, classical music refers to music created in Europe roughly between 1750 and 1820. It includes the works of Franz Joseph Haydn, Wolfgang Amadeus Mozart, and Ludwig van Beethoven. Today, however, classical music usually refers to many kinds of **Western** music from many different eras. Classical music includes operas, **chamber music**, and music played by symphony orchestras.

# CHAPTER 2

# A PARIS CHILDHOOD

A street scene in Paris, France. This photo was taken in 1955, the year Yo-Yo was born.

Yo-Yo Ma was born in Paris, France, on October 7, 1955. His parents were both musicians who had come to Paris from China to continue their music studies. Ma's father, Hiao-Tsiun, was a violinist, composer, and professor of music. His mother, Ya-Wen, had trained as an opera singer.

## BETWEEN TWO CULTURES

Hiao-Tsiun Ma was born near Shanghai in 1911. He loved music from an early age and learned to play the violin. By the time he was in his twenties, he knew he wanted a career in music, but the political situation in China interfered with his plans. China had been politically unstable throughout Hiao-Tsiun's childhood. In the 1930s, the country was suffering from a civil war and an invasion by Japanese troops. Many well-educated Chinese were leaving the country and going to Europe and other places in the West. In 1936, Hiao-Tsiun decided to leave China. He went to Paris to study and lived there throughout World War II (1939–1945). Hiao-Tsiun did not return to China until after the war, when he was offered a teaching position at Central University (now called Nanjing University) in Chongqing.

Ma's mother, Ya-Wen Lo, was born in Hong Kong in 1923. Like Hiao-Tsiun, she was devoted to music, and her ambition was to become an opera singer. She was studying music and voice at Central University when World War II ended. Hiao-Tsiun, who had returned to China to teach at the university, was Ya-Wen's professor of music theory.

Hiao-Tsiun had looked forward to returning to China, but the political situation was still very dangerous. China was torn again by civil war. The ruling party, the Chinese Nationalists, were battling the **communists** for control of the country. In 1949, Hiao-Tsiun returned to Paris, and Ya-Wen left China for France the same year. They became reacquainted in Paris and were married there on July 17, 1949. By December of 1949, the communists had succeeded in taking control of China. The couple remained in Paris, where their first child, a girl named Yeou-Cheng, was born in 1951. Yo-Yo followed four years later.

When Yo-Yo's parents were growing up, China was a place of great political turmoil.

In Paris, the Ma children grew up in two cultures. They spoke French at school and Chinese at home. Music became their third language, and it filled the family's tiny apartment. To anyone who knew Hiao-Tsiun and Ya-Wen's love of music, the Ma's musical household was no surprise.

## AN IMPORTANT EDUCATION

Life in Paris was not easy for the Mas. When Yo-Yo was born, the family was living in a one-room apartment. Hiao-Tsiun earned a small allowance as a student at the University of Paris. He gave music lessons on the side to earn extra money. The family also received financial help from Hiao-Tsiun's brother, Hiao-Jone Ma, who was living in the United States. Although Ma's parents were not wealthy, they made sure their children received a good education. Hiao-Tsiun taught the children the Chinese language and Chinese **calligraphy**. He also gave them lessons in French and French history. He loved teaching, especially when it came to music.

This child in Shanghai, China, is learning Chinese calligraphy. With the help of his father, Yo-Yo also learned how to write the intricate characters.

Both children showed a talent for music at a very young age. Yeou-Cheng learned to play the piano at age three and began violin lessons with her father soon afterward. Yo-Yo also began piano lessons at three. Before long, he, too, expressed a desire to learn a string instrument. But he did not want to play the violin.

Instead, telling his parents he wanted to play something "big," he chose the double bass—the largest instrument he had ever seen. Believing the instrument was too big for a four-year old, Hiao-Tsiun brought home a cello for his son instead. Yo-Yo was delighted.

## One Piece at a Time

Hiao-Tsiun Ma loved nothing better than teaching. One reason Yo-Yo and his sister were able to learn so much so quickly was their father's teaching method. Hiao-Tsiun knew that learning anything difficult can be overwhelming for a child – a child can easily become tired, bored, or completely uninterested. To make learning easier for his children, Hiao-Tsiun came up with a plan. He broke everything down into small pieces.

Learning a Bach cello **suite** is a challenging task for any cellist, especially a four-year-old. Hiao-Tsiun made the task easier by having Yo-Yo learn just two measures of the music each day. By the end of two days, Yo-Yo knew four measures, and by the third day, he knew six. People were amazed that a four-year-old could play Bach, but for Yo-Yo, learning the suites was not difficult. As he once told an interviewer, "When a problem is complex, you become tense, but when you break it down into basic components you can approach each element without stress." Hiao-Tsiun applied the same teaching method to other subjects. Yo-Yo mastered Chinese calligraphy by learning two characters a day. With French, he memorized a paragraph of text each day. Hiao-Tsiun was patient, but he was also strict. He told his children that achieving any goal requires hard work and discipline.

This young cellist is about the same age Yo-Yo was when he made his first public concert appearance in Paris, France.

It soon became apparent that Yo-Yo was a **prodigy**. He could learn a piece of music, commit it to memory, and play it to perfection almost immediately. With his father's help, Yo-Yo learned his first Bach cello suite at age four, and he could play three Bach suites by the time he was five. That same year, he gave his first public concert in Paris. He played both the cello and the piano, and he dazzled his audience.

German composer Johann Sebastian Bach has had a tremendous influence on modern musicians and composers, including many outside of the classical music world.

## Bach and the Cello Suites

The music of German composer and organist Johann Sebastian Bach (1685-1750)—considered one of the giants of Western music—has always been an important part of Yo-Yo Ma's life. Bach's cello suites were the first pieces Ma learned to play, and he has continued to perform them throughout his career. He has recorded the suites twice and used them as the basis for a film series called "Inspired by Bach."

Bach was famous for using counterpoint, which means two or more melodies being played at the same time. With the cello suites, Bach attempted something revolutionary. The cello is a single-melody instrument—it plays one note after another to create a single melody. But in Bach's cello suites, notes are played simultaneously, and listeners hear more than one melody line at one time.

The music of Bach also has special meaning to Ma because of its connection to his father. When Hiao-Tsiun Ma lived in Paris during World War II, one way that he kept up his spirits was to memorize Bach pieces for the violin and play them to himself at night, in the dark. Later, Hiao-Tsiun patiently taught Yo-Yo the cello suites in their Paris apartment. Yo-Yo was at his father's bedside when he died in 1991. His father's last request was to hear his son play Bach's fifth cello suite.

# CHAPTER 3

One day in 1962, a letter arrived at the Ma's apartment in Paris. The letter was from Hiao-Tsiun's brother in the United States. He wrote to say he wanted to move back to China. Hiao-Tsiun couldn't believe what he was reading. China was still a communist country, and his brother would never have the same opportunities there as he did in the United States. Hiao-Tsiun believed he had to go to the United States and convince his brother to stay. The Mas took their life savings and headed for New York. They planned to stay for only six months. Once in the United States, however, Hiao-Tsiun saw all the opportunities that existed for his own children. Not only did he persuade his brother to remain, but he convinced himself to stay. The family settled in New York City.

This photograph of New York City shows the skyline as it appeared in the early 1960s, when the Ma family moved to New York from Paris.

## A Lifelong Dream

Hiao-Tsiun decided to stay in New York for the sake of his children, but the move also allowed him to fulfill a lifelong dream of his own—the founding of a children's orchestra. Hiao-Tsiun founded the Children's Orchestra of New York in 1962. It provided children of all economic backgrounds with training in classical music as well as opportunities to perform. Yo-Yo and his sister Yeou-Cheng were among the eighteen members of the original orchestra. They are still involved in the orchestra today. Now called the Children's Orchestra Society, it operates under the direction of Yeou-Cheng and her husband. Yo-Yo serves on the Artistic Advisory Board.

Composer and conductor Leonard Bernstein (left) enjoyed working with young musicians. He is shown here in 1963, conducting a nationally televised concert with sixteen-year-old Andre Watts at the piano. Watts remains one of America's most celebrated pianists.

The opportunities that Hiao-Tsiun imagined for his children materialized quickly once the family was settled in New York. A friend visiting the Mas heard Yo-Yo play and was amazed by his talent. He arranged for Yo-Yo to meet the renowned cellist Pablo Casals, who was living in New York at the time. Casals was just as impressed and looked for a way to introduce the young boy to a wider audience. He found the perfect opportunity. On November 29, 1962, Yo-Yo and his sister Yeou-Cheng played at a benefit concert in Washington, D.C., for the city's Cultural Center (now the Kennedy Center of the Performing Arts). The famous American composer Leonard Bernstein was conductor and Master of Ceremonies. U.S. president John F. Kennedy and his wife Jacqueline were in the audience. The seven-year-old Yo-Yo played the cello, while his sister accompanied him on the piano. The concert was broadcast on national television.

## TRUSTED TEACHERS

Even a prodigy needs a **mentor**, and Yo-Yo was lucky to have several. Soon after the Ma family arrived in New York, Hiao-Tsiun hired the noted cellist Janos Scholz to instruct Yo-Yo. Legendary violinist Isaac Stern was also helpful. He had heard Yo-Yo play in Paris, and even then he knew he was witnessing something special.

# Pablo Casals

Pablo Casals (1876–1973) was one of the greatest cellists of the twentieth century. His career spanned nearly a hundred years. He performed at the White House for President Theodore Roosevelt in 1904, at the age of twenty-eight, and for President John F. Kennedy in 1961, at the age of eighty-five. Casals did more to popularize the cello than any previous player.

A Spaniard, Casals fled Spain in 1939 when **dictator** Francisco Franco took control of the country at the end of the Spanish Civil War. Thousands of other Spaniards also fled the country and were living in refugee camps in France. Casals spent much of his time delivering food and clothing to fellow refugees. He continued aiding refugees of the Spanish Civil War throughout his life. Casals believed strongly in peace, freedom, and human rights. Yo-Yo Ma said of him, "He saw himself not primarily as a cellist but as a musician, and even more as a member of the human race."

Ma admired Casals for his ability to express deep emotion through his playing. He was also impressed by Casals's stamina. When Ma was sixteen, he played in an orchestra under Casals's direction. Ma recalls, "I'll never forget the way his mind and body would radiate vitality the moment he raised his baton. That was an inspiration for a lifetime." Casals was ninety-five at the time.

Stern recommended Yo-Yo to his friend Leonard Rose. Rose had been principal cellist with the New York Philharmonic and was now teaching at the Juilliard School of Music. He gladly took on Yo-Yo as a new pupil. Rose nurtured the boy as well as the musician. The outgoing Rose helped Yo-Yo to loosen up and gain both courage and confidence.

Pablo Casals conducts a rehearsal of the Marlboro Festival Orchestra in Marlboro, Vermont, in 1971. Even when he was in his nineties, Casals was an energetic conductor.

Leonard Rose was a distinguished cellist with the Cleveland Symphony Orchestra and the New York Philharmonic before he devoted himself to teaching.

In Paris, Yo-Yo had been used to living in two cultures, but adjusting to life in the United States was difficult. Yo-Yo's Chinese heritage demanded strict obedience and discipline, but Americans valued freedom and self-expression. "As soon as we moved to America I had to deal with two contradictory worlds. At home, I was to submerge my identity. You can't talk back to your parents—period. At school, I was expected to answer back, to reveal my individuality." Ma struggled to find his place. When he turned thirteen, the urge to rebel was strong. "My home life was totally structured. Because I couldn't rebel there, I did so at school." Yo-Yo was enrolled at the Professional Children's School in New York City, a special school for secondary and high school students who have careers in the performing arts. Yo-Yo would often wander the city streets instead of going to class. He missed so many classes that his teachers became worried. They assumed he was bored, and they put him in a more difficult, accelerated program. Despite his rebellious ways, Yo-Yo did well enough in the program to complete his high school education when he was only fifteen.

After graduating from high school, Yo-Yo thought about college. His sister Yeou-Cheng was studying at Radcliffe College, located near Harvard University in Cambridge, Massachusetts. Ma considered going to Harvard to be close to his sister. In the end, however, he decided to spend the next year in New York City, where he could continue his studies with Leonard Rose while taking college courses at Columbia University.

## LETTING GO

The summer following his high school graduation, Yo-Yo attended Meadowmount, a summer camp for string players in New York's Adirondack Mountains. It was the first time he had been away from home. It was also the first time he had been with so many other young musicians. Yo-Yo was thrilled to be in their company. "There was always music in my family, but I grew up pretty lonely. The first time I was among kids who loved music was at Meadowmount ... I was 15 and when they wanted to play Beethoven in the middle of the night I went nuts. It was so exciting."

The Adirondack Mountains in northern New York state provide the backdrop for Meadowmount, a summer camp for string musicians. There, far away from New York City and the discipline of home life, the fifteen-year-old Yo-Yo felt free for the first time in his life.

For the first time in his life, Yo-Yo felt truly free. It showed in his behavior—he wrote graffiti on the walls, and at one point he left his cello outside in the rain. It also showed in his music. He later recalled, "That summer, I played the Schubert Arpeggione **Sonata** and the Franck Sonata with uninhibited freedom—just letting go, in a way that had never happened before."

When Yo-Yo returned to New York City that fall, Leonard Rose was pleased to see him playing with more emotion and imagination than ever before. He encouraged Yo-Yo to experiment. In the past, Rose had always helped Yo-Yo analyze a new piece of music before playing it. Now Rose allowed him to learn new pieces on his own. He let Ma come up with his own ideas as to how a piece should be played. Ma was grateful for Rose's trust. "One of the hardest things a teacher can do is to give a student permission to go his own way. I'll always be grateful to Mr. Rose for that."

## AN IMPORTANT DECISION

While Yo-Yo's cello playing was enjoying a new, creative phase, his college courses at Columbia were suffering. He began cutting classes again, and he eventually dropped out of school altogether. He spent most of his time hanging out at Juilliard, where Rose still taught.

Yo-Yo was only a teenager, and in many ways his struggle against discipline was typical teenage behavior. Still, Yo-Yo Ma was no ordinary teen. By the age of fifteen, he had appeared on the television program *The Tonight Show*, played at Carnegie Hall, and performed as a soloist with the San Francisco Symphony. He was already being compared to the greatest cellists of the century. At the age of sixteen, Yo-Yo found himself at a crossroads, one not faced by most young people. He could devote the next few years to studying music and performing around the world, or he could continue his education at a college that offered more than just music classes. Yo-Yo chose the latter route, and in the fall he enrolled at Harvard University.

Yo-Yo Ma studied at the Juilliard School in New York City. Founded in 1905 to provide high-quality musical training for American musicians, the school later expanded to include training in dance and drama.

The Juilliard School

# A TIME OF GROWTH

# CHAPTER 4

Ma did not realize it at the time, but his decision to go to Harvard would have a profound impact on his life. Isaac Stern, who knew Ma since he was a child, once said, "During those growing years—whatever growing pains there were—Yo-Yo made a decision rather remarkable for a talented young man of his age, and that was to try to get an education. He could have devoted all his time to preparing pieces for concerts and competitions, but he took the unusual step of deciding to become a person."

Harvard University in Cambridge, Massachusetts, introduced Yo-Yo Ma to new worlds beyond music. Ma once said, "Harvard has everything to do with my trying to stretch boundaries. My Harvard experience informs my life to this day."

## THRIVING AT HARVARD

When Yo-Yo Ma arrived at Harvard in the fall of 1972, he was ready for all it had to offer. Musically, he blossomed. His teachers recognized his extraordinary talent but knew he could be even better. They pushed and challenged him. They taught him to analyze music in new ways. It wasn't enough to know that a piece of music excited him. Why was it exciting? When learning a new piece, Ma no longer looked at the cellist's part first. Now, he studied the whole **score**. This larger perspective made music-making much more interesting.

While Ma was at Harvard, he received many offers to perform with professional orchestras. During his freshman year alone, he played thirty concerts all over the world. He had so many offers that year that at one point he considered leaving school. His father convinced him to stay, and he has never regretted his decision.

For the next three years, Ma limited himself to one out-of-town concert a month. That allowed him to become more involved in the social and musical life of Harvard. He made himself available for all kinds of musical opportunities, whether it was playing in the orchestra for a school musical or simply playing in the living room of a dormitory. He also played chamber music with other students, and their concerts at Harvard's Sanders Theater became very popular. One of his roommates, a pianist who often performed on campus with Ma, remembered, "We played a lot in Sanders Theatre, and even back then, the word was out about

While a student at Harvard, Yo-Yo Ma often performed at Sanders Theater, located on the campus.

this phenomenon, and there were never enough seats. One of my enduring images is Yo-Yo inviting a crush of people, who couldn't get tickets, into the transept of Memorial Hall [outside the theater] at about 7:30 and playing Bach suites for them, right up to the moment he had to go on stage."

## NEW PASSIONS

Ma's enthusiasm for learning was not limited to music. He took a full load of academic courses—everything from astronomy to Russian literature. He would call other students in the middle of the night to talk about the Russian writer Fyodor Dostoevsky. Ma admits that he could carry a full course load in addition to his musical performances because he didn't worry about getting perfect grades. He just wanted to learn as much as possible. His favorite subject was **anthropology**. It stimulated his curiosity about people and other cultures. In particular, he was excited by a class in which he studied the people of the Kalahari, a desert region in southern Africa. Fascinated by their culture, he became determined to visit the region one day.

While at Harvard, Ma spent his summers at the Marlboro Music Festival in Marlboro, Vermont. Founded in 1951, the festival gives young musicians the chance to study and perform with some of the foremost professional musicians in the world. Ma made many lasting friendships during his summers at Marlboro. He met pianist Emanuel Ax there in 1973 and they have been close friends and musical collaborators ever since.

Ma began another lasting relationship at Marlboro. During his first summer there, he met a festival administrator named Jill Hornor. The two discovered they had much in common. Like Ma, Jill played a string

instrument—she was a violinist—and she had also lived in Europe for many years. By the end of the summer, Ma was in love. He kept in touch with Jill over the next several years, despite frequent and distant separations, and in 1977 the couple married.

Yo-Yo Ma and his wife Jill attended the opening of Walt Disney Concert Hall in Los Angeles, California in October 2003.

In 1978, at the age of twenty-three, Yo-Yo Ma was awarded the Avery Fisher Prize, America's highest award for musical achievement.

## BECOMING A FULL-TIME CELLIST

Ma graduated from Harvard in 1976 and began a full-time career as a cellist. In 1978, he won the prestigious Avery Fisher Prize, which is perhaps the highest honor in the United States to be given to a musician. After Ma married Jill Hornor, they settled in a suburb west of Boston. Neither of them imagined how busy Ma's career would become. Offers to perform came pouring in, and Ma found it hard to say no. He traveled constantly, playing over one hundred concerts each concert season. He didn't slow down until 1983, when his son, Nicholas, was born. Ma realized he had to put family first, and he cut back on the number of concerts he played. Three years later, he and Jill had a second child, a daughter they named Emily.

Despite a reduced touring schedule, Ma's fame as a cellist continued to grow. Between 1983 and 1989, he recorded over twenty-five albums and won five Grammy Awards. By the end of the 1980s, Ma had established himself as one of the premier cellists of the twentieth century. He earned that reputation playing traditional classical music from Western countries. In the 1990s, he would step out of that world and venture into brand new territory.

## A Risky Operation

In 1980, Ma underwent an operation that could have ended his career as a cellist. Ma had a condition called scoliosis, which is a curvature of the spine. His cello playing may have made his condition even worse. When he was twenty-four, his doctors warned him that if he didn't have an operation soon, the condition might become permanent. If nerves were damaged during the operation, however, there was a chance that Ma would never be able to play the cello again. Ma and his wife prepared themselves for that outcome. As Ma told an interviewer, "Long before the operation, I was prepared for the possibility that it might not turn out successfully. I had decided that there's more to life than the cello. There are so many things that I would find enormously exciting. I love people; perhaps I'd do social work, or become a teacher ... "

Fortunately, the operation was a success. But recuperating was slow. Ma had to spend the next six months in an upper-body cast. He cut back on his performances, but he eventually resumed a full touring schedule.

# CHAPTER 5

# STRETCHING BOUNDARIES

By 1990, Ma had been out of college for fourteen years. As the decade progressed, however, the seeds that were planted during his years at Harvard began to bear fruit. His anthropology and history classes, as well as his collaborations with people outside the music world, all had an impact on the course his career was about to take. Over the next ten years, Ma would stretch the boundaries of classical music and travel the world in search of new musical adventures.

Yo-Yo Ma became fascinated with the Kalahari Desert in Africa while enrolled in an anthropology course he took at Harvard.

## BEYOND CLASSICAL MUSIC

In 1993, Ma finally fulfilled his dream to visit the Kalahari Desert in Africa. This desert covers a vast region within the countries of Botswana, Namibia, and South Africa. It is a harsh, barren land where, until recently, many ways of life remained unchanged for thousands of years. Ma was interested in learning about the music of the Kalahari. His guide and translator introduced him to a group of local musicians. Ma played Bach for them on his cello. He was surprised to find that Bach's music, which had always seemed old to him, suddenly felt modern when

## A Unique Collaboration

It is common for a singer to be accompanied by a pianist. For a singer to team up with a cellist is unusual, but that is what happened when Yo-Yo Ma and jazz vocalist Bobby McFerrin got together. Like Ma, McFerrin grew up surrounded by classical music. Both of his parents were singers. His father, Robert McFerrin, Sr., was the first African American male soloist at the Metropolitan Opera in New York.

Bobby McFerrin has a unique singing style. He enjoys **improvising** and can make his voice sound like an instrument. When Ma and McFerrin began working together, Ma had to learn how to improvise. It was difficult, even scary, at first. But with time and help from McFerrin, the two found a way to mesh their musical styles. They had so much fun doing it, they decided to record an album. *Hush* was released in 1992. The album is a mixture of classical pieces and original songs by McFerrin. Despite the novelty of such a duo, the album was a commercial success and sold over a half million copies. It was the number one album on Billboard's Classical Crossover charts for thirty-three weeks.

Jazz vocalist Bobby McFerrin's distinctive singing style combined with Yo-Yo Ma's classical cello playing to create the hit crossover album *Hush* in 1992.

played in the midst of their ancient culture. Ma then listened to his hosts play. He was fascinated by their instruments. Made of commonplace materials such as twigs and fiber, they looked so simple. As Ma soon discovered, however, playing them was not easy. Ma picked up a venturo, which, of all the instruments, seemed the most similar to a cello. It was basically an oil can with a metal string and a wooden bow. Ma struggled to coax a pleasing sound from it and everyone had a good laugh. By the end of his visit, Ma knew that he wanted to learn to play many different kinds of music.

## EXPLORING APPALACHIA

Yo-Yo Ma became interested in Appalachian music the first time he heard American fiddler Mark O'Connor play. Ma was so impressed, he went backstage immediately after the concert and said, "Can you teach me?" Ma wanted to learn to play his cello in the style of Appalachian fiddle music. Appalachian music is folk music from the Appalachian mountain region, which stretches from New York to Alabama. The music has its roots in Europe, particularly the British Isles. Many of the people who settled the mountainous region came from Ireland and Scotland, and they brought their fiddling traditions with them. Though fiddling styles have changed over the years, the early settlers' swinging music for jigs and reels (two kinds of dances), as well as their gentle ballads, are still characteristic of Appalachian music.

Ma and O'Connor arranged to meet at least once a month. They were joined by double-bassist Edgar Meyer. Both Meyer and O'Connor had played everything from classical to jazz to bluegrass. Ma could not have found two better musicians to lead him into the world of American folk music. The problem for Ma, however, was the difficulty of learning to play this music. It had a much faster tempo, or speed, than what Ma was used to in classical music, and the lively melodies required extreme precision. Ma needed many sessions with O'Connor and Meyer before he felt comfortable.

In 1996, the trio recorded an album called *Appalachia Waltz*. The album contains some traditional American songs, but most of the music was written by O'Connor and Meyer. These new songs combine elements of folk and

Fiddler Mark O'Connor (left), bassist Edgar Meyer (middle), and Yo-Yo Ma kicked off their *Appalachian Journey* tour at the Grand Ole Opry in Nashville, Tennessee, on March 30, 2000.

classical music. The three musicians teamed up again in 2000 to record a second album, *Appalachian Journey*. Popular singers James Taylor and Alison Krauss made guest appearances on the album, and they also joined Ma, O'Connor, and Meyer in a series of sold-out concert performances. *Appalachian Journey* went on to win a Grammy Award for best crossover album. Like its predecessor, it crosses the boundaries between folk and classical music.

## READY TO TANGO

In 1997, Ma journeyed to South America. His destination was Argentina—the land of the tango. Tango music was born in Buenos Aires, Argentina, at the beginning of the twentieth century. At the time, millions of European immigrants were crowding into the port city. They brought their musical traditions and instruments with them. The music that emerged was a combination of European melodies and African rhythms. Early tango bands contained just three instruments— a violin, a piano, and a bandoneon, which is similar to an accordion.

## Inspired by Bach

Ma has wandered far from classical music, but he has never left it completely. In the mid-1990s, he returned to Bach's six cello suites—the same suites he had studied as a child in Paris. Ma had recorded the suites once before, in 1983. He now recorded them again, but this time they were accompanied by film. Ma has always been interested in how music affects people, including nonmusicians. For his new project, he asked a variety of artists to each create a work based on one of the Bach suites. The result would be recorded on film, one film for each suite. Ma called his project "Inspired by Bach." The artists involved included filmmakers, a **choreographer**, ice skaters, a Japanese **Kabuki** actor, and even a garden designer. The films show the creative process from beginning to end and include conversations between the artists and Ma about how the music inspired them.

When the films were released, they were not well received. Classical music fans complained that the visuals detracted from Bach's music. Others thought the project was nothing more than Ma showing off. For Ma, however, the films were a genuine reflection of his belief that music is not just for musicians and that everyone can take meaning from, and respond to, music. Despite the criticism, Ma was happy he did the project. "One of the most interesting aspects of the film project was collaborating with so many people. ... For me, working together with all those idealistic, dedicated people constituted a second college degree. ... It made me an infinitely richer person, and I think a better musician. No matter what people said about the project—and it raised a lot of eyebrows—I'll never regret having done it."

For his film project "Inspired by Bach," Yo-Yo Ma asked Olympic gold medalists Jayne Torvill and Christopher Dean to choreograph a figure skating dance to the music of Bach.

Ma was drawn to Argentina because of the music of a bandoneon player named Astor Piazzolla (1921–1992). Piazzolla composed some of the most sophisticated tango music ever written. When he was born in Argentina in 1921, tango was flourishing. His family moved to New York City when he was four. They stayed for ten years—long enough for the young Piazzolla to study classical piano and fall in love with American jazz. Back in Argentina, Piazzolla played the bandoneon in tango orchestras. In the 1940s, he began composing his own music, but most people hated it! His tangos, which contained elements of jazz and classical music, were too complex for most audiences. Even more shocking for the time, he wrote concert pieces that put the

Argentine tango musician and composer Astor Piazzolla playing the bandoneon in 1974

Moves such as this one are typical of the tango, which caused an uproar when it first appeared.

## Tango Fever

Tango music inspired the tango—a dance that also originated in Argentina. The dance alternates between slow steps and sudden turns, and it is full of dramatic poses. When the tango arrived in Europe, just before World War I (1914–1918), it caused a sensation. Many considered it scandalous because partners had to dance so close to each other. Tango fever soon spread to the United States, and young couples everywhere took to the dance floor. There were tango bands in restaurants and ballrooms, and people had tango parties in their homes. The tango craze hit its peak during the 1920s, especially after actor Rudolph Valentino danced the tango in the 1921 film *The Four Horsemen of the Apocalypse*. People still dance the tango today, but it is mostly performed by professional dance troupes or ballroom dancers. Latin America has produced other popular dances, such as the rumba and the cha-cha, but the tango was the first dance craze to sweep the Western world.

bandoneon in the middle of a traditional string orchestra. It took decades for Piazzolla's music to be appreciated.

Most people don't associate the cello with tango, but Piazzolla included the instrument in his arrangements. Of particular interest to Ma was a piece Piazzolla wrote for cello and piano called "Le Grand Tango." Ma has said that when he first heard it, "The music caught me like a fever and wouldn't let go." Although Ma had never played tango, the musicians he met in Argentina were eager to share their enthusiasm for Piazzolla's music. In 1997, Ma and these musicians recorded an album of Piazzolla's music called *Soul of the Tango*. It was Ma's first venture into Latin American music and it won a Grammy Award for Best Classical Crossover Album.

Antonio Carlos Jobim (1927–1994), pictured below, was a Brazilian composer and pianist. He popularized bossa nova, a musical style that combines the Brazilian samba and American jazz. Several of his compositions appear on Yo-Yo Ma's Brazilian album *Obrigado Brazil.*

## Bound for Brazil

In 2003, Ma returned to South America, this time to explore the music of Brazil. Like tango music, Brazilian music is a mixture of African and European (especially Portuguese) influences. In Brazil, Ma rejoined many of the musicians he had worked with on the tango project. Together, they recorded an album called *Obrigado Brazil*, which means "Thank you Brazil" in Portuguese. The album celebrates the full range of Brazilian musical styles, including the samba, the bossa nova, and two pieces by Brazil's foremost classical composer, Heitor Villa-Lobos (1881–1959), who happened to be a cellist.

# THE SILK ROAD REBORN

# CHAPTER 6

Yo-Yo Ma traveled many new musical roads in the 1990s. His longest and most ambitious journey began in 1998 when he founded the Silk Road Project. The project takes its name from the "Silk Road," an ancient trade route that linked Asia and Europe. Camel caravans traveled the route carrying items such as tea, spices, and gold—and precious Chinese silk. The Silk Road was active from between about 200 B.C. and A.D. 1500. Stretching from the Pacific Ocean to the Mediterranean Sea, the Silk Road was actually a network of different routes that crisscrossed the mountains and deserts of Central Asia. Ma's Silk Road Project covers the same vast territory.

The Silk Road stretched for thousands of miles, crisscrossing Central Asia and forming a link between China and Europe.

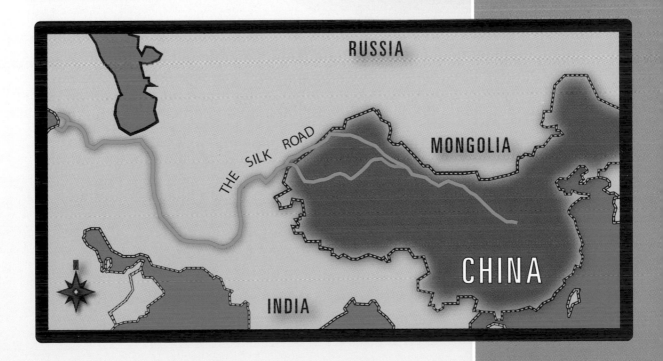

Kabul, the capital city of Afghanistan, was a major trading stop along the ancient Silk Road.

Ma's idea for the Silk Road Project developed gradually. The more he traveled, the more curious he became about the different cultures—and kinds of music—that he encountered. He began wondering if there were connections between these different cultures and musical forms. He found himself asking, "Could we actually do research and find vibrant traditions linking different parts of Asia, linking Asia and the West, linking past and present, that we didn't yet know about?"

Such links are the key to Ma's vision for the project. The old Silk Road connected people from diverse backgrounds. Ma hopes this project will do the same. Many of the peoples and cultures that lined the original route still exist. The Silk Road Project seeks to reconnect them through music rather than trade.

It is easier to make musical connections than political ones, but the exchanges brought about by the Silk Road Project may help people understand each other better. As Ma explains, "In our world where people seem

### A Chinese Heritage

Like the Silk Road, Yo-Yo Ma's life reflects a mixture of different influences, and these influences include his own Chinese heritage. "I'm fascinated by Chinese history and the complexities of Chinese culture," he has said. "I love Chinese art, and ... I value the traditional Chinese veneration of wisdom and learning."

## The "Internet of Antiquity"

Yo-Yo Ma has compared the Silk Road to the modern internet, calling the Silk Road the "internet of antiquity." The Silk Road provided the first global exchange of information. People who lived and traveled along the route shared knowledge and ideas. Cultures mixed and information flowed back and forth, shrinking the distance between China and Europe. As is the case with today's internet, there was plenty of buying and selling on the Silk Road. Shipping by sea gradually replaced the legendary overland route. While it prospered, however, the Silk Road was indeed the internet of antiquity.

increasingly interested in finding their own identities, their cultural roots, sometimes we can get into trouble by saying my roots have no connection with your roots and therefore we're separate. But if we uncover the knowledge which shows that in fact there are connections ... this can be very liberating and incredibly valuable for cross-cultural understanding."

## NEW VOICES, ANCIENT CULTURES

For Ma, an obvious way for people to connect is through music. At the core of the Silk Road Project is the Silk Road Ensemble, a group of young musicians who come from many different countries. The instruments and music these musicians play reflect the great diversity of the Silk Road Project. A performance by the ensemble might feature traditional songs from Mongolia, China, or Iran. It might even include a classical piece written by a Westerner who was influenced by the East. The musicians perform on traditional instruments, but much of the music they play is new. When Ma formed the Silk Road Ensemble, he wanted to celebrate tradition but move forward as well. He has commissioned many new pieces for the ensemble so that new, young voices have a chance to be heard.

In 2001, Ma and the Silk Road Ensemble recorded an album called *When Strangers Meet*. The music reflects the many cultures along the Silk Road. The group has performed throughout Europe, the Far East, and the United States. In May 2003, the musicians toured Central Asia, where much of the music they play originated. At every stop, they gave **master classes** and met with local musicians and students. In Kazakhstan, Ma even played with a local rock band. When the ensemble arrived in Kyrgyzstan, Ma was granted honorary citizenship. He gave his acceptance speech in perfect Kyrgz, the local language.

Ma is both a friend and a mentor to the other members of the ensemble. Wu Man, a Chinese lute player, told a reporter, "Ma is like a big brother to us. He's the greatest communicator I have ever met. He is able to

Ma performing with the Silk Road Ensemble in New York City in 2002. Wu Man, the musician on the far right, is holding a Chinese instrument called a pipa.

use his music to create connections between people, and teaches us to listen to each other better both as musicians and human beings."

## A Friendly Horse

To Westerners, Asian music is full of unusual sounds. Just as unusual are the instruments that make those sounds. When Ma began the Silk Road Project, he was intrigued by a Mongolian instrument called the *morin khuur*, or "horse-head fiddle." The name is derived from the horse's head carved at the top of the instrument. Like a cello, the morin khuur is played with a bow, but it has a square body, and there are two strings instead of four. Ma was eager to learn to play the morin khuur, but it took a long time to master it. As he once said, playing an instrument with fewer strings "doesn't make it twice as easy."

It seems fitting that Ma was drawn to the horse-head fiddle. The name "Ma" means "horse" in Chinese. "Yo" means "friendly." In learning to play the morin khuur, one horse befriended another!

A Mongolian musician plays the morin khuur, or horse-head fiddle. The top of the instrument is carved in the shape of a horse's head. The strings of the instrument, as well as the bow, have traditionally been made of horsehair.

### REACHING BEYOND MUSIC

Ma's goals for the Silk Road Project include more than just music. He has brought together scholars, artists, choreographers, and others to promote all kinds of cultural exchanges. The Silk Road Project has partnered with museums around the world to showcase the art

Yo-Yo Ma greets Huang Binggen of China at the Peabody Essex Museum in Salem, Massachusetts. The Huang family's ancestral home, a two-hundred-year-old Chinese merchant's house, is now on display at the museum as part of a creative exchange sponsored by the Silk Road Project.

and architecture of the countries along the historic route. Museums involved in the project also offer a variety of educational programs, lectures, and workshops in craftmaking and storytelling.

## A BOLD EXPLORER

Ma calls the Silk Road Project the most exciting thing he has ever done. The project reflects his own past: growing up in several cultures, exploring history and anthropology, learning different types of music, and collaborating with others. It also reflects his personality. Ma is a bold explorer. He enjoys crossing boundaries, befriending strangers, and sharing knowledge.

Ma signing CDs at a music store in California. Ma's popularity reaches across generations, cultures, and musical styles.

## Ma on Film

In 2000, the film *Crouching Tiger, Hidden Dragon* hit movie screens worldwide. An epic tale set in nineteenth-century China, it wowed audiences with its thrilling martial arts and exotic setting. The film's music was as haunting as the scenery, and it won an Academy Award for best original score. Tan Dun, a native of China, composed the music, which uses both Chinese and Western instruments. Yo-Yo Ma appears on the soundtrack, playing the cello as well as several traditional Chinese instruments. Like the Silk Road Project, the film's soundtrack is a blend of East and West, combining Asian tones and Western harmonies.

Ma can also be heard on the following film soundtracks:
- playing the music of Beethoven in *Immortal Beloved* (1994)
- playing the music of John Williams in *Seven Years in Tibet* (1997)
- playing tango music in *The Tango Lesson* (1997)
- playing the music of Philip Glass in *Naqoyqatsi* (2002)
- playing a Bach cello suite in *Master and Commander* (2003)

# CHAPTER 7

# A GENEROUS SPIRIT

Ma teaches master classes whenever and wherever he can. Here, he listens to a high school student during a master class in Taiwan in May 2000.

Yo-Yo Ma's talent has made him one of the most honored musicians in the world, but it is his generosity that has endeared him to so many people. Ma is always looking for opportunities to share what he has learned. When he tours, he makes time to meet and work with young musicians. He gives master classes as often as he can.

Like his father, Ma enjoys working with children. He has appeared on the television shows *Sesame Street* and *Mister Rogers' Neighborhood*, as well as the animated children's television show *Arthur*. Perhaps because he has two children of his own, Ma likes being around kids. With young musicians, his manner is gentle and encouraging. He listens intently and offers advice in terms they can understand. During a master class in Minneapolis, Minnesota, Ma suggests to an eleven-year-old boy that he will get a fuller sound from his cello if he pushes his bow, really follows through with it, as if he were throwing a ball. At another master class, in Cambridge, Massachusetts, a student asks Ma what she should do if she gets tired in the middle of playing a long piece. Ma tells her, "Use the power of the orchestra to help you, that's the secret."

## WINNING ISN'T EVERYTHING

Many music students feel compelled to enter competitions, but Ma is against competitions and refuses to be a judge at them. He once explained his reasons to an interviewer: " ... first of all, you have to compare people; that's bad enough. Then, you have to judge them by points, which means dissecting something organic, and denying an artistic person the chance to turn a weakness into a strength. And think how many contestants have to lose so that one may win!"

In music, as well as in life, Yo-Yo Ma is a firm believer in experimenting, learning, and sharing.

The pressure on young musicians can be intense. Those young people who spend all of their time practicing and performing may see little of the world outside the concert hall. Such a way of life concerns Ma. "I believe the years between 15 and 20-something are essential to your development; everything you learn during that time is there for you to draw on the rest of your life. If you put all your energy into performing instead of trying to open yourself to experimenting and learning different ways of making music, you'll be a diminished person. And exploring, finding the depth of your own soul and other people's, that's what music is all about."

## "Joy from Music"

It is difficult to make a living as a professional musician. There are few spots available in symphony orchestras, and competition for those spots can be fierce. Ma worries that students focused on a music career may forget they have other options. "They go to music school and nobody tells them what's out there. They should be prepared to work with other people, teach, contribute to their community, even to apply the discipline and knowledge they've acquired to some other fields and still derive joy from music." Ma could be describing his sister Yeou-Cheng. A talented violinist, she decided not to pursue a career in music. Instead, she attended medical school and became a doctor. She has contributed to music, however, through her work with the children's orchestra that her father, Hiao-Tsiun Ma, founded.

## THE IMPORTANCE OF BEING FEARLESS

Yo-Yo Ma believes that the emphasis in music should not be on success or failure. It should be on learning and participating. Students should be encouraged to take chances and not worry about turning each experience—or performance—into a success. "It doesn't matter if you fail," Ma has said. "What does matter is that you tried."

As for Yo-Yo Ma, he will certainly continue to take chances. His boundless energy and curiosity will lead him on new musical journeys. Luckily for the rest of us, he will take his audience along with him.

## Ambassador to the World

Many people already think of Yo-Yo Ma as a musical ambassador. Now he is an official ambassador for CultureConnect, a program supervised by the U.S. Department of State. The program was created following the terrorist attacks of September 11, 2001. Its goal is to promote dialogue and understanding among the world's diverse cultures. CultureConnect ambassadors such as Ma serve as teachers and mentors to young people throughout the world. In December 2003, CultureConnect sponsored a concert in Washington, D.C., in which Ma performed with the Iraqi National Symphony Orchestra. The concert marked the first time the Iraqi musicians had performed in the United States.

Yo-Yo Ma rehearses with the Iraqi National Symphony Orchestra in December 2003.

# TIMELINE

| | |
|---|---|
| **1955** | Yo-Yo Ma is born on October 7 in Paris, France |
| **1959** | Begins playing the cello at the age of four |
| **1961** | Gives first public recital in Paris, playing both cello and piano |
| **1962** | Ma's father moves the family to New York City; Yo-Yo and his sister appear on national television with Leonard Bernstein |
| **1964** | Begins studies with Leonard Rose at Juilliard School of Music in New York City; appears at Carnegie Hall and on *The Tonight Show* with his sister |
| **1970** | Appears as a soloist with the San Francisco Symphony |
| **1972** | Spends the first of four summers at Marlboro Festival in Vermont |
| **1976** | Graduates from Harvard University |
| **1977** | Marries Jill Hornor |
| **1978** | Receives Avery Fisher Prize |
| **1984** | Wins first Grammy Award for Best Classical Performance, Instrumental Soloist or Soloists (Without Orchestra) for *Bach: The Unaccompanied Cello Suites* |
| **1991** | Receives an honorary doctorate from Harvard University |
| **1993** | Visits the Kalahari Desert in Africa |
| **1996** | Records *Appalachia Waltz* |
| **1997** | Records *Soul of the Tango* |
| **1998** | Founds the Silk Road Project |
| **2000** | Records *Appalachian Journey*, which wins Grammy Award for "Best Classical Crossover Album" |
| **2001** | Records *When Strangers Meet* with Silk Road Ensemble; Ma is awarded the National Medal of the Arts, the United States' highest honor for artistic excellence |
| **2003** | Records *Obrigado Brazil*; performs in Washington, D.C., with the Iraqi National Symphony Orchestra |
| **2004** | Wins sixteenth Grammy Award, for *Obrigado Brazil* |

**anthropology:** the study of people, especially their origins and cultures.

**bossa nova:** Brazilian music that emerged in the 1950s and combines elements of samba (an earlier form of Brazilian dance music) with elements of jazz.

**calligraphy:** the art of creating elaborate, elegant handwriting.

**chamber music:** instrumental music written for a small group of musicians.

**choreographer:** a person who creates dances, usually by directing dancers.

**commissioned:** requested that something be created, such as a work of music.

**communists:** people who believe that a government should own all or most private property and should control the economy.

**dictator:** a leader who has absolute control over a country.

**improvising:** playing spontaneously invented variations of a musical theme.

**Kabuki:** traditional Japanese theater that features dancing and singing.

**master classes:** music classes for advanced students, taught by a master musician.

**mentor:** a person that someone trusts to provide guidance or instruction.

**pitch:** in music, the highness or lowness of a note, corresponding to a particular frequency of sound waves.

**prodigy:** a highly talented young person.

**range:** in music, the extent of notes an instrument or voice can produce, from the lowest pitch to the highest pitch.

**repertoire:** the supply of dramatic or musical works that can be performed.

**score:** in music, the written or printed form of a particular musical composition.

**sonata:** a musical work composed for one or more solo instruments.

**suite:** a work of music that consists of several related but different pieces.

**virtuoso:** a person who is highly skilled at something, such as playing music.

**Western:** having to do with Europe or places settled by Europeans.

# TO FIND OUT MORE

## BOOKS

Burgan, Michael. **Marco Polo: Marco Polo and the Silk Road to China (Exploring the World)**. Minneapolis: Compass Point Books, 2002.

Chippendale, Lisa. **Yo-Yo Ma: A Cello Superstar Brings Music to the World (People to Know)**. Berkeley Heights, N.J.: Enslow Publishers, 2004.

Ganeri, Anita. **The Young Person's Guide to the Orchestra**. New York: Harcourt, 1996.

Kallen, Stuart A. **The History of Classical Music (Music Library)**. San Diego: Lucent Books, 2002.

Levine, Robert T. **The Story of the Orchestra**. Minneapolis: Black Dog & Leventhal, 2000.

Stevens, Kathryn. **Cellos**. Chanhassen, Minn.: Child's World, 2002.

Vernon, Roland. **Introducing Bach (Introducing Composers)**. Broomall, Pa.: Chelsea House, 2000.

## INTERNET SITES

**Astor Piazzolla**
*www.piazzolla.org*
Includes a biography, an interview, an opportunity to listen to recordings, and links to related sites.

**CultureConnect**
*http://cultureconnect.state.gov*
Information about the program and photographs of Ma's performance with the Iraqi National Symphony Orchestra.

**Historical Cellists**
*www.cello.org/cnc/cellold.htm*
Information about many important cello players of the past, including Pablo Casals.

**The J.S. Bach Home Page**
*www.jsbach.org*
A biography, information on his complete musical works, and links to related sites.

**The Silk Road Project**
*www.silkroadproject.org*
The Silk Road Project's official web site.

**Yo-Yo Ma**
*www.yo-yoma.com*
Yo-Yo Ma's official web site.

# INDEX

## INDEX *(continued)*

## About the Author

**Susan Ashley** has written twenty-five books for children. She has always loved music and has had the pleasure of seeing Yo-Yo Ma perform live. She has fond memories of listening to Leonard Bernstein's Young People's Concerts as a child, as well as her parents' bossa nova records. Today, her CD collection includes everything from Greek music to rock music, and opera to bluegrass. Susan lives in Wisconsin with her husband and two cats, who don't seem to mind her eclectic musical tastes.